The Art, Science and Law of Business Succession Planning

**O'NEIL CANNON
HOLLMAN DEJONG & LAING** s.c.

MILWAUKEE · PORT WASHINGTON · GREEN BAY

Copyright © 2018
O'Neil, Cannon, Hollman, DeJong & Laing S.C.

All rights reserved.
No part of this book may be reproduced in any form
or by any means without permission in writing from the publisher,
except for brief quotations embodied in critical articles and reviews.

For information or to order additional copies, contact
O'Neil, Cannon, Hollman, DeJong & Laing S.C.
111 E. Wisconsin Avenue
Suite 1400
Milwaukee, Wisconsin 53202
414.276.5000
www.wilaw.com

ISBN 978-1-719-30459-7

Book Design by
Scott Johnson, Scotnik Press

First Edition, May 2018

Table of Contents

Introduction 1

Chapter 1: The Need for Succession Planning 7

Chapter 2: The Five Objectives of Good Succession Planning 13

Chapter 3: Objective 1-Maximizing the Value of the Business 17

Chapter 4: Objective 2-Minimize Taxes 25

Chapter 5: Objective 3-Provide for the Continuity
and Survival of the Business 33

Chapter 6: Objective 4-Treating Your Children Equitably 39

Chapter 7: Objective 5-Preserving Family Harmony 49

Chapter 8: Seven Pitfalls that Work Against a
Successful Transition 53

Chapter 9: What a Good Succession Planner Will Do 61

Chapter 10: Structuring Buy-Sell Agreements 69

Chapter 11: The Key Employee Agreement 89

Epilogue 101

About Our Law Firm 103

Disclaimer 107

Introduction

IT'S THE LARGEST CORPORATE RESTRUCTURING IN AMERICA. It's happening right now, as you read these words.

It will continue for several decades. Before it ends, it will involve nearly half the nation's work force, which generates an estimated 40 percent of the Gross Domestic Product.

It's the millions of family-run businesses–from corner shops to conglomerates–that are collectively undergoing the nation's largest transfer of ownership, as ownership passes from one generation to the next.

According to the Conway Center for Family Business, about 78 percent of new job creation in the United States stems from family-owned businesses of all sizes. Small businesses alone account for more than 50 percent of the American workforce. That's a huge piece of the economic pie in America—yet with many of these business owners getting ready to retire, it is unclear how the pie will be divided in coming years. Estimates suggest that only 30 percent of these businesses will successfully transfer ownership to the next generation, and just 12 percent will make it to the third generation.

Introduction

Further data underscores the potential resulting economic disruption to owners and employees. A 2015 survey by Baker Tilly International, a global network of independent accounting and business advisory firms, revealed four out of five family businesses were not "succession-ready." A 2016 survey by US Trust of Americans with at least $3 million in investable assets, revealed 63 percent of business owners have no formal exit strategy for when they leave their companies.

These statistics are unacceptable— customer lists, products, intellectual property, trade secrets, reputation and goodwill are all valuable. The family business is a treasured asset that should bring income and benefit to your family and subsequent generations. With careful and methodical succession planning, it can.

It won't happen automatically, though. You must be purposeful in your approach. Hence, we wrote this book.

Six Questions Every Family Business Owner Should Be Asking

If you own a family business, you should be thinking about your succession plan, whether you plan to sell the business to fund your own retirement or pass it on to your descendants or other key employees. To get you started, here are six questions to ask yourself:

- *Am I prepared to consider transferring <u>ownership</u> of my business during my lifetime?* If you ever plan to retire—if you don't intend to die at your desk —you should already be thinking about this. Will you retain ownership in the business, draw retirement or hand it over completely?

- *Am I prepared to consider transferring <u>control</u> of my business during my lifetime?* Ownership and *control* are different things. Do you have mechanisms in place so the business can run effectively in your absence?

- *Have I made sure that the transition of my business will be orderly?* If the answer is currently "no," expect chaos during the transition, unless you make a plan.

- *Is there a logical successor to me in the management of the business?* Who among your family members or employees has the qualifications to lead the business when you leave it? If no one comes to mind, whom could you groom to take over?

- *Are my key employees comfortable with my plans for business continuation, and will they stay with my firm rather than seeking more secure employment?* If you don't want your best employees working for your competitors—or becoming your competitors—down the road, you need to take appropriate steps to answer this question in the affirmative.

- *Is my estate sufficiently diversified so that children who are not active in the business may be treated fairly*

Introduction

alongside those receiving an interest in the business? Not all your children will want a role in your company, but you want all of them to benefit from your wealth. How will you structure your estate to accomplish this goal?

Six Keys to Successful Business Succession

As you ponder the six questions above, you'll begin to grasp the importance of succession planning—but truthfully, you need more than just a healthy understanding or respect for the process. Any successful business transition also requires:

- Willingness among the retiring generation to turn over responsibility and authority to the successors.

- Well-groomed successors who possess most of the founder's skills for running the business.

- Accommodative heirs who agree to work together for the common good of the business.

- Willingness among family or key employees to seek objective, professional help whenever needed.

- Workable business plans that outline goals for the company and responsibilities of the successors or heirs.

- Early estate planning that recognizes the financial needs of each generation, with an eye toward reducing tax burdens.

In the pages ahead, we'll give you some guidance to help you find answers to the six questions above, as well as suggestions on putting in place all six of the required ingredients for a successful transition.

We'll open with a more in-depth discussion of why you need a good succession plan and when to begin the process. We'll provide a list of important objectives to be met, then expand on each objective with a dedicated chapter, offering practical methods for you to meet each goal. We'll conclude by offering important advice on structuring some of the most important legal documents you'll need to make your succession plan ironclad.

By the end of this book, you should have a much clearer understanding of the succession planning process, and you will be well on your way to securing your company's, and your family's, financial future.

Chapter 1

The Need for Succession Planning

"Why do I need succession planning?"
"Can't I just hand my business over to my children?"
"Why can't I just leave the business to someone in my will?"

AS A LAW FIRM FOCUSED ON HELPING BUSINESS OWNERS plan for the succession of their businesses, we hear these questions, and others like them, all the time. We understand. After spending decades dealing with all the details of a successful family business, the last thing many business owners want to do is handle more details. When the time comes, they wish they could just wave a wand, instantly transfer their company to someone else, and not think about it anymore.

Unfortunately, that's not how it works. Until you've actually completed the transfer of your business to someone else, the details of the exchange are yours to deal with— and if you don't spell out the transition clearly, you leave the door open for unexpected results.

Think of it this way: You've put years into building this business. You've invested time, money, blood, sweat and tears, and that investment is now paying off. Your business provides well for your family, and you want it to continue doing so for many years to come, long after you retire, long after you pass away. For this to happen, at some point you must give control of the business to a successor, whether a family member or an outsider.

The only way to do this safely is through succession planning. Isn't your investment worth protecting through the vulnerabilities of succession, even if it means a few more details along the way?

Succession Planning Is a Process, Not an Event

Many people think of transferring a business as a one-and-done event. In reality, effective succession planning begins years before the transfer actually occurs (hence the "planning" part).

Once the plan is in place, as your life and business evolve, you may need to make updates and changes to the plan, until the time comes to pass the business to your successor.

Challenges Involved with Succession Planning

Succession planning can be challenging; there are often a few difficulties along the way. That is why we advise business owners to begin thinking about, and planning for, succession as early as possible. There are two basic reasons why succession planning can be difficult:

1. *You must attempt to predict future events with as much accuracy as possible.* Of course, none of us can know the future; we can only predict it. Succession planning requires you to predict you'll be ready to retire at a given age, for example, and your successor will be prepared to take over management or ownership of the business when you're ready to transfer it. You'll also need to anticipate as many variables as possible. What happens in the event of a health crisis, a natural disaster or a financial hit? What happens if your appointed successor dies? What happens if a successor divorces and remarries? A good succession plan forecasts one outcome, but it remains flexible to account for other possible outcomes, as well. Developing a succession plan that achieves this balance requires careful forethought and attention to detail.

The Need for Succession Planning

2. *In a family owned business, you must account for emotions and attitudes, not just facts and figures.* Everyone associated with the business will present some sort of emotional variable, and every decision you make concerning your business may touch on those emotions. You must take into account the emotions of close and extended family members, as well as the emotions of your employees and associates who must work under new management or owners. Even your own emotions will come into play as you weigh these decisions.

Succession Planning Involves Multiple Layers

For most business owners, "succession" involves more than just handing the reins to someone else. You'll need to address questions of ownership and management of the company, both of which may occur at different times:

Ownership succession planning usually intertwines with your estate planning, because your business is part of your estate.

Management succession planning addresses who will run the company when you step down—whether it's a family member, a key employee or someone else.

You can see how quickly succession can become complicated and convoluted. A well-constructed plan can avert many of these complications before they derail the process and give you peace of mind, knowing you have "the bases covered."

Before moving forward with our discussion, we understand that some business owners may choose to sell their business outright, instead of passing it to a family member. In cases like these, succession planning becomes simpler; you work out the details of liquidating the organization and incorporating the proceeds into your estate plan. Having said that, for our purposes, from here on out, we're going to presume your goal is to keep your family business "in the family," with ownership going to future generations. We'll share how to do this successfully in the pages ahead.

CHAPTER 2
The Five Objectives of Good Succession Planning

NOW THAT WE'VE ESTABLISHED WHY YOU NEED a well-constructed succession plan for your business, let's talk briefly about five essential objectives the plan needs to address. The five objectives are:

1. Maximize the value of the business
2. Minimize taxes
3. Provide for the continuity and survival of the business

The Five Objectives of Good Succession Planning

4. Treat your children equitably
5. Preserve family harmony

As you can imagine, meeting all five of these goals is a balancing act. For instance, you may entertain several strategies for maximizing value and ensuring the business's survival, but not all of these will preserve family harmony. You'll have to weigh some decisions against others (possibly over and over again), before arriving at a strategy that meets all five objectives.

Objective 1: Maximize the Value of the Business

Since this probably has been the goal of your business all along, succession planning simply shifts this strategy to the context of continued growth and value once you're no longer at the helm.

Objective 2: Minimize Taxes

Without proper planning, income and estate taxes can take a huge bite out of your business. Your advisor can present options, structures and strategies to reduce this burden significantly.

Objective 3: Provide for the Continuity and Survival of the Business

You'll need to balance a number of dynamic factors here, including the current direction of the economy and key staff and family members involved with the business. Additionally, if you want to sign over the business to one or more of your children *before* you pass on, you need to consider your financial security and standard of living, based on your company's profitability. You may also want to include a component that provides for your own continued compensation.

Objective 4: Treat Your Children Equitably

Typically, business owners want all their children to receive equitable benefit from their business or estate, regardless of the children's ownership stake or level of involvement in the company.

Objective 5: Preserve Family Harmony

Questions of succession and inheritance always carry the potential to evoke conflict between family members. Some may feel entitled to particular parts of your estate, while others may feel slighted by your decision to give control to someone else. This objective can sometimes be the most difficult to meet, but careful planning and open discussion make it possible.

Consider the Needs and Goals of All Affected Parties

Bear in mind that everyone with "skin in the game" brings needs and goals to the table, and you'll need to take these into account in your plan. These affected parties include:

1. You (the owner) and your spouse
2. Children who are active in the business
3. Children who are not active in the business
4. Key management staff who are not family

The Five Objectives of Good Succession Planning

With this reality in mind, we encourage honest discussion with all affected parties throughout the process, from planning to the actual transfer. These conversations may be challenging at times, but open conversation is almost always preferable to keeping people in the dark and then surprising them.

Your People Come First

Tax considerations and other financial factors are a necessary part of all business planning, but remember the *best interests of your family and key people always outweigh tax considerations*. Tax savings alone should never be the deciding factor for a specific plan.

Finally, as you strive to meet and balance these five objectives, remember that *you may have more alternatives than you see at first*, which is where your attorney's advice comes in handy. Don't get discouraged as you work through the issues. As long as you keep these objectives in mind, your options are limited only by the imagination, current laws, and your commitment to the plan being carried out.

CHAPTER 3

Objective 1:
Maximizing the Value of the Business

EVERY BUSINESS—NO MATTER HOW LARGE, small or financially sound— becomes vulnerable to losing value during a change of leadership. Thus, your first goal with succession planning should be to enact a strategy that enables the company to preserve its value and continue to grow after the transfer is complete.

For our discussion, we will assume you've already built a

Objective 1: Maximizing the Value of the Business

profitable family business that remains on a growth trajectory. The guiding principles that have built your success won't change; the primary variable is the transfer itself. Thus, your best strategy for maximizing company value is to protect its value during the transition. For that reason, this chapter focuses mainly on protection strategies.

Developing and Retaining a Trusted Management Team

Your best defense against losing company value is to assemble a strong management team well in advance. This team may consist of family members or key associates or managers you trust.

For any key management people who are non-family, it is wise to incentivize them by giving them some financial stake in the company's operation. Consider the following examples.

Minority Stock Ownership

One of the more common methods of sharing a financial stake with key management personnel is to grant them a minority interest in the company through stock ownership. Though if you do so, bear in mind that, by taking this action, you're giving these managers more than just a vested interest-- you're also granting them specified rights and legal access to the company as minority stockholders. Let's address some of these in turn.

Right of Inspection

At any time, stockholders have the right to inspect and make copies of some corporate documents, including the list of stockholders, the stock ledger and some financial records. To view or copy these documents, the stockholder must make a written demand stating a "proper purpose" for doing so. In Wisconsin, state law defines "proper purpose" as "a purpose reasonably related to such person's interest as a stockholder."

In plain English, the law requires you to make these records available to minority stockholders if the stockholder provides a specific reason why it's pertinent to their investment. This does not mean you have to automatically open all of your books for every request. If a stockholder requests to see the corporation's books and records, the burden of proof is on the stockholder to demonstrate why this information is needed.

On the other hand, stock ledgers and stockholder lists are more in the stockholder's domain, and the burden of proof would be on you to show why that member does not have a "proper purpose."

Right to Bring a Derivative Suit

If a minority stockholder believes it necessary, he or she may have the legal right to file a "derivative lawsuit"—that is, to sue a third party on behalf of the institution in which he or she owns stock. These suits don't happen often, but you need to know they can happen.

Derivative suits are intended to let a stockholder to protect his investment in the corporation in the event that the firm's leadership fails to do so.

Thus, a third party defendant may be any entity who poses

Objective 1: Maximizing the Value of the Business

a perceived threat to the company's wellbeing. That includes its executive officers and directors. In an extreme application, if you make a key employee a stockholder while you remain in an executive position, that employee could subsequently sue you on behalf of the company, if he or she believes you breached your duties in some way (such as by using corporate property for personal gain).

In most cases, the stockholder can only bring a derivative claim if the following conditions are met:

- The stockholder must meet the minimum standing requirements as a stockholder, based on applicable laws. (For example, he or she must own a specified number of shares or be stockholder at the time of the alleged offense.)

- The stockholder must have already made a written demand to the board of directors to take action, and the board either refused or failed to act.

Because the derivative claim is filed on the company's behalf (rather than the individual stockholder's), if he or she wins the case, any financial award goes to the corporation, and not directly to the stockholder.

Right to Protection Against Shareholder Oppression

This provision protects minority stockholders against financially oppressive or harmful actions by stockholders with a controlling share in the corporation. Examples include:

- Controlling shareholders buy more shares below fair market value

- Forcing minority shareholders to sell their shares below market value

- Taking actions that cause minority shares to drop in value significantly

If a minority stockholder believes controlling stockholders are committing shareholder oppression, he or she may file a direct suit against the corporation itself, as opposed to a derivative suit.

When you maintain good relations with key employees, and when your company conducts business in an upright manner (even in your absence), chances of a minority stockholder invoking these rights are greatly reduced. But because you grant these rights to anyone who has stock ownership, choose your stockholders wisely.

Deferred Compensation/Bonuses

If you don't want to face the complexities involved with minority stock ownership, deferred compensation can also be an excellent way to give a financial stake to non-family members of your management team.

Deferred compensation is additional income paid out over time, based on profits or other identifiable goals. This gives your key employees a great incentive to stay with your company post-succession. You can implement deferred compensation in a variety

Objective 1: Maximizing the Value of the Business

of ways; we generally review four of the most common types below.

Deferred Bonus Plans

Bonus plans provide excellent incentives to work hard and grow the company, because the workers receive a share of the additional profits. When bonuses are deferred, they can incentivize staff to remain with the company as long as possible. For example, if you calculate bonuses annually, an employee could receive 50 percent up front, 25 percent in year two and 25 percent in year three, with additional annual bonuses adding to the amount each year. With this in place, employees know they will forfeit a portion of their bonus if they leave the organization.

Non-Qualified Retirement Plans

Unlike the standard plans defined by the Employee Retirement Income Security Act (ERISA), a non-qualified retirement plan is a tax-deferred instrument designed for the specific retirement needs of key employees.

Under this structure, an institution agrees to pay specified additional compensation to the employee upon retirement, and this amount is calculated according to a vesting schedule. Thus, the longer the employee stays with your company, the larger this retirement bonus will be, up to a fixed amount.

Stock Appreciation Rights (SARs)

With stock appreciation rights (SARs), your key employees receive additional deferred compensation tied directly to firm growth. As your business increases in value, your employee's financial stake grows proportionately in the form of ownership shares, based also upon the employee's tenure with the company. These shares are given to the employee upon one or more "triggering events," such as when the employee retires, or if the business is sold.

Phantom Stock Plans

Phantom stocks are similar in nature to SARs, with the main exception that they aren't actual stock, but instead stock "units" that parallel the value of real stocks. Upon a triggering event as described above, the non-family employee receives a dividend or cash bonus for her phantom stocks, proportionate to the increased value of the actual stock.

Non-Compete Agreements

When a key employee leaves, your company's value may become vulnerable. This is especially true if that employee has knowledge of your client base or trade secrets. To preserve your business interests, you'd be wise to have these employees sign a non-compete agreement of some sort. These agreements occur in two basic forms:

- *Non-compete Clause (or, Restrictive Covenant):*
  Under this agreement, the employee promises that if he or she leaves the organization, he or she will not perform similar work that might compete with your business within a defined geographic range, for a set period of time.

Objective 1: Maximizing the Value of the Business

- *Nonsolicitation Agreement:* This agreement specifies that an employee leaving the company will not attempt to solicit your clientele away from you.

Non-compete agreements are validated by some sort of *valuable consideration*—that is, an added value to the employee as an incentive to sign. For an employee just coming on board, the valuable consideration may be the job offer in itself; however, if you ask existing key personnel to sign a non-compete, you'll need to include additional incentives, such as a bonus, a raise or increased benefits.

It is important to note that in Wisconsin, the validity of non-compete agreements is determined on a case-by-case basis, so it's critical to consult with an employment lawyer regarding the specifics of these contracts.

As the owner of your business, you've already developed habits that encourage company growth. By utilizing tools such as those we've described above, you're building a trusted, motivated management team and laying important groundwork for continued growth of your business after you leave it.

CHAPTER 4

Objective 2:
Minimize Taxes

WE'RE STATING THE OBVIOUS HERE, but just to keep it top-of-mind:

Every dollar you spend in taxes is a dollar your beneficiaries won't see.

The more you minimize your tax burden, both on your business and your estate, the more benefit your loved ones receive from your hard-earned wealth.

Objective 2: Minimize Taxes

Your business doesn't just pay taxes; it is also a taxable asset in and of itself as part of your estate. Thus, for this chapter, we're going to expand our discussion beyond succession planning to talk more broadly about estate planning in general, particularly with regard to how estate asset structuring affects taxation.

At the time of this writing, if an individual dies with an estate valued at $11.2 million or less, all of the individual's assets will be exempt from estate taxes. The $11.2 million figure is called the "basic exclusion amount," because it represents the maximum value of assets that can be gifted during the taxpayer's lifetime and/or at his death without being subject to gift or estate taxes. The basic exclusion amount is indexed for inflation, meaning under current law it should increase based on inflation rates. The tax savings is achieved by a maximum tax credit in the amount of tax on the first $11.2 million of the individual's taxable estate. We'll refer to this credit as the *"unified* tax credit," because it represents a credit for gifts the taxpayer made during his or her lifetime and upon his or her death, collectively. If the estate's value exceeds the basic exclusion amount, then the value of the assets over that threshold is taxed at 40 percent.

For a married couple, each spouse is able to claim this unified tax credit. That's a combined $22.4 million in assets that can be passed on tax free.

Note that many estate planning attorneys recommend being conservative when dealing with the unified tax credit, cautioning clients to proceed on the basis of a lesser amount being subject to the credit. The debate in Congress over the value of the basic exclusion amount, and therefore the amount of the unified tax credit, is ongoing. Estate plans need to be reviewed and adjusted depending on changes in the law.

Regardless of the exact amounts of the basic exclusion amount and unified tax credit, the point is that you can reduce the size of your estate and by extension the amount of tax owed through strategic gift giving. Families often use this strategy to transfer a portion of their wealth to their children before passing on, especially considering the tax savings. Let's look at two ways you can use gifts to minimize taxes.

Lifetime Gift Exclusion

As we said, the unified tax credit applies to the first $11.2 million a taxpayer gives away during his or her lifetime, at death, or through a combination of lifetime and post-death gifts. This means that the current basic exclusion amount of $11.2 million (indexed for inflation) includes the value of gifts made during the taxpayer's lifetime and at death, collectively.

If your business or other investments have the potential to appreciate significantly in coming years, your estate will grow accordingly. Making larger lifetime gifts and using part of your basic exclusion amount during your lifetime may be an effective strategy to moderate the tax burden on this growth.

Annual Gifts

By law, you're allowed to give annual gifts up to $15,000 per recipient without being charged a gift tax. You can give up to $15,000 per year to as many different individuals as you like,

Objective 2: Minimize Taxes

and these amounts do not count against your basic exclusion amount.

Therefore, under this rule, you may give each of your children $15,000 every year tax-free, thus reducing the size of your estate, and without tapping into your basic exclusion amount.

Additionally, your spouse can also give up to $15,000 – so you can actually double your annual gift per recipient (through a technique called "gift splitting" by filing IRS Form 709.

Fully Utilizing the Unified Credit

Because the unified tax credit can potentially save millions in taxes, your estate planning documents should be drafted to ensure full utilization of this credit for each spouse. Your business interests may require a bit of restructuring to take full advantage of this credit, which is where succession planning can help.

As stated earlier, each spouse has an individual unified tax credit, so collectively, a married couple may claim exemptions from estate and gift taxes on combined estates worth up to $22.4 million.

If your business is classified as what is called "deferred marital property," and the non-titled spouse dies before the titled spouse, there may be insufficient assets to fund the family trust or otherwise utilize the surviving spouse's unified credit. A marital property agreement can solve this by re-classifying all or part of the business interests as marital property or the non-titled spouse's individual property.

Business Succession Planning

To illustrate the point, let's say your parents own an estate, including real estate, business assets and other property, worth $14 million total. They own these assets jointly with the right of survivorship: When one of them dies, all shares of those assets automatically transfer to the surviving spouse. Let's say that your father passes away, and now your mother has all $14 million in assets to herself.

This isn't a problem for Mom, directly, but it means that the value of her estate now exceeds her individual $11.2 million unified credit. Once she passes away, the $2.8 million will be left unshielded by her credit and therefore be hit with the 40 percent federal estate tax.

With planning, that situation may be averted. Let's take a closer look.

Transfer tax law says spouses may transfer assets to each other without having to pay transfer taxes. This benefit stems from the marital deduction, which means transfers between spouses do not count toward the transferor's unified credit.

To understand this concept better, let's say that instead of jointly owning property, your parents decide to divide ownership between them: Your mom will own a country farm, and your dad takes ownership of a lakeside cottage set on 50 acres, and so forth. Each of them now separately owns assets worth $7 million.

Alternatively, they could change the real estate assets from joint tenancy to "tenancy in common." This would mean that both spouses own a half interest in each piece of property, without any rights of survivorship.

OBJECTIVE 2: MINIMIZE TAXES

Next, their wills or trusts can be written in such a way that their unified credits can shield the estate from transfer taxes. As an example, instead of leaving the entire lakeside property to your mom, your father could leave the cottage to you and your siblings: This prevents your mom's estate from exceeding her unified credit.

Now, if your mother wants to retain some control over the lakeside property, she can still do that through other mechanisms, such as a "life estate." In a life estate, a deed includes a reservation that, for the remainder of her life, she can use the cottage however she likes–live in it, collect income from it, rent it out, pay property taxes on it, etc.–but ownership has technically passed to you and your brothers and sisters. Therefore, she has all of the use and enjoyment of the property, but it is no longer in her estate as a taxable asset.

Double Basis Step-Up

When the first of two spouses dies, it's important to ensure that the basis of the surviving spouse's interest in the business will be "stepped up." This action enables the surviving spouse to sell the business with no additional income tax cost.

Why is this strategy important?

According to Internal Revenue Code Section 1014(a), for any capital asset you receive from somebody who decedent paid for it, but instead based on "the fair market value of the property at the date of the decedent's death." The recipient's tax basis in the asset is "stepped up" (or down) to the fair market value of the asset as of the date of death. This can help if the asset is later sold for a profit, because it is likely less of the profit will be considered taxable gain.

Essentially, this provision means that any appreciation in the business's value during the first spouse's lifetime doesn't have to be subject to capital gains tax, a potentially significant tax savings to the recipient of the business interest(s).

This is crucial because most married couples own much of their holdings jointly with right of survivorship. When one spouse dies, all the assets pass to the surviving spouse. For couples with smaller estates, the unified tax credit shields them from paying state or federal death taxes. However, in larger estates, or those containing assets that increase significantly in value, the transfer of ownership can trigger significant capital gains taxes when those assets are eventually sold. This is where the step-up in basis provision can be very powerful as a tax-savings tool.

Therefore, the step-up in basis rule allows the surviving spouse to moderate potential taxes by "stepping up" the basis of assets transferred at the first spouse's death: the tax basis is set at the time the surviving spouse took ownership of the asset, rather than the time it was first acquired.

Tax Strategies for Life Insurance Proceeds

Life insurance plays a very important role in succession planning, as we will explore in detail in the following chapter. Proceeds

Objective 2: Minimize Taxes

from life insurance policies are generally excluded from income tax if they are owned personally. However, if your corporation owns the policy, it may pay taxes indirectly on these proceeds.

At least two strategies may be implemented to avoid this possible taxation:

1. Structure your company as an S-corporation; or

2. Set up a "split-dollar life insurance" plan, with the corporation named as the owner of the cash surrender value, while the business owner (or someone else) is the beneficiary.

The strategies discussed above represent just a few of the more common ways you can structure your succession and estate planning to minimize the tax burden on your family and your business. Because tax laws constantly change, you should periodically revisit your plan to ensure that your tax structures are still relevant and that you are taking full advantage of all available tax savings.

CHAPTER 5

Objective 3:
Provide for the Continuity and Survival of the Business

IF EVERYTHING IS GOING AS IT SHOULD, you have yet to see the full potential value of your business. If everything continues to go the way it should, you never will.

It sounds paradoxical, doesn't it?

Why has your business not reached its full potential? It's not that business is bad, necessarily, or that you've got problems, but

Objective 3: Continuity and Survival

rather that your business should keep growing and thriving long after you've passed the torch, long after you've passed away. The value of your business today is a fraction of what it could be worth 10 or 20 years from now. Smart succession planning acknowledges that even a well-established family business is still a work in progress, an *appreciating asset*. One of your primary goals, then, is to plan for your company's long-term survival, so your descendants can benefit from it for many years to come. Let's discuss some methods by which you can accomplish this goal.

Assembling a Strong Team

Building a strong management team to survive the owner's death or retirement is key to the successful continuation of the business. These can be family or non-family members, depending on the factual situation. In Chapter 3, we discussed some ways to incentivize your team by giving them a financial stake in the company, but that's only part of the equation. You also want to choose members of your management team based on key criteria:

1. *Adherence to the company's vision and guiding principles.* To perpetuate your business's success, your succession team must be fully committed to the standards and culture that helped you achieve that success in the first place.

2. *Adherence to sound financial practices.* Your successors must understand and practice the company's approach

to finances to maintain an environment of sustainability and growth.

3. *An eye for the future.* While you want a team that appreciates and follows your established best practices, you also want people who are forward-thinking, people who adapt to the ever-changing culture of business and will make necessary changes that keep your company vibrant and relevant.

Life Insurance

Life insurance can play a major role in navigating a successful transition and securing the future of your business. For one thing, life insurance is an economically efficient funding vehicle for meeting a potential liability. For another, it is generally tax-free. Below are some examples of creative ways you can incorporate life insurance into your plan.

Paying Estate Taxes

Because it is tax-free, life insurance proceeds can be used to pay estate taxes at less than half the cost of any other method.

In many cases, you can plan for payment of estate taxes using life insurance by setting up an irrevocable life insurance trust (ILIT). The ILIT owns your life insurance policy (or policies), therefore keeping it out of your estate and making it exempt from taxes. Upon death, the proceeds then are designated to pay any estate taxes.

Objective 3: Continuity and Survival

This method can be highly effective for covering growing business assets that, over time, may push the value of your estate past the exemption threshold.

Substitute for a Taxable Asset

Life insurance can also be a tax-free substitute for a specific taxable asset that is subject to estate taxes— for example, the increased value of your company.

Provide Key Man Coverage

You can obtain an insurance policy, life and/or disability, to cover significant financial losses in the event a key member of your team ("key man") dies or becomes otherwise incapacitated.

Capital Infusion

Life insurance can be structured to provide needed capital infusion, either to reduce debt or increase working capital.

Fund a Buy-Sell Agreement

If your business operates under a buy-sell agreement in which the company is required to buy out a partner's interest upon death, you can utilize life insurance to pay for the buyout. The death benefit is paid to the partner's surviving family.

However, it's important to note that if life insurance is used to fund a buy out of a deceased owner's interest, the insurance proceeds may be exposed to the claims of corporate creditors.

Because of this risk, corporations may prefer cross purchase agreements with other shareholders.

Redemption of Owner's Stock

Finally, in the event your family either leaves or liquidates the company, life insurance can provide funding for redemption of the owner's stock for estate liquidation.

With the right management team in place, combined with a life insurance structure tailored to your company's needs, you can establish important safeguards that can help your company survive and thrive long after you move on. Once you've put these structures in place, review them periodically and make adjustments as your company continues to evolve.

CHAPTER 6

Objective 4:
Treating Your Children Equitably

MERRIAM-WEBSTER'S DICTIONARY DEFINES the word *equitable* as "having or exhibiting equity: Dealing fairly and equally with all concerned." In the context of succession planning, "dealing fairly and equally" doesn't necessarily require that everyone gets precisely the same sized piece of the pie. Rather, it means

[39]

Objective 4: Treating Your Children Equitably

everyone involved is given the same fair consideration in a manner suited to him or her.

When it comes to transferring the business and other assets to one's children, the business owner has three options:

1. *Treat the children unequally.* For instance, the owner leaves 100 percent of the business to the one child who has been active in running the business, while leaving remaining assets, usually of a much lesser value, to the other children. This is often perceived as "unfair," and will usually cause family dissension.

2. *Treat the children equally by leaving undivided interests in all assets.* This can ultimately destroy a business, because non-active children who assume control of the business may make decisions which are in their best interests, and not necessarily in the best interest of the business itself.

3. *Divide asset value equally, but allocate business assets to involved children.* See to it that children active in the business end up with ownership and/or control of the business, while ensuring the other children are still treated substantially equally.

Of these three options, the third is the fairest and most equitable, and it offers many methods of implementation. We'll spend the remainder of this chapter exploring some of these methods.

Asset Segregation

The owner may opt to leave distinct assets to different children, thereby avoiding undivided interests. This approach presents four potential challenges:

1. *The values of the relevant assets may change.* Although perhaps equal when the plan is created, by the time the children inherit the property, the specific asset values may be substantially unequal.

2. *The assets may no longer be in the estate at the death of the parents.* Certain assets considered in the initial plan may have been sold prior to the decedent's death and the proceeds applied to other assets, causing a distribution imbalance.

3. *The amounts of loans and mortgages against specific properties may constantly change.* The shifting values may affect the ultimate value of each asset.

4. *Assets left to one child may be essential to the continued operation of the assets now belonging to another child.* This scenario, of course, may become a source of friction.

To deal with the challenges stated above, an asset plan separating specific assets must be constantly updated to maintain equality.

One way to solve these problems is to split only the assets that the owner believes he or she will retain until his or her death.

Objective 4: Treating Your Children Equitably

The goal is to equalize the values at the inception of the succession plan (with life insurance as an equalizer if needed), and leave any other assets not already included in the plan by will.

By valuing the business at inception of the plan, you allow those in control of the business (i.e., your active children) to be either rewarded with its growth or to suffer any devaluation that occurs between your transfer of ownership and your death. For your children not active in the business, you give them other assets (possibly insurance), either by gift during your lifetime or by will upon your death. These other equalizing assets could be equal in value to the value of the business at the time it is transferred to the active children. Additionally, an interest factor could be added to reflect the time value of money.

Minority Interest Gifts Coupled with a Buy-Sell Agreement

The goal of this combination of structures is to transfer ownership of the business to your children in an equitable manner, while enabling future adjustments in the equity distribution. You can accomplish this strategy in three steps:

1. *For your children currently active in the business,* give a gift of stock to compensate them for their efforts so far.

2. *At this point,* treat all the children equally, giving more stock to the children in the business and other assets to those who are not.

3. *Create a buy-sell agreement.* In the agreement, the corporation can redeem the stock or allow the other children working in the business to purchase stock either at death or during the owner's lifetime. If a redemption is used in a family owned business, the owner must consider the dividend/capital gain alternatives (§ 302(b)(3) of the Internal Revenue Code) and the need to waive family attribution (I.R.C. § 302(c)).

Option to Purchase Stock

If you don't like the ideas of asset segregation or making gifts of stock requiring stock purchase agreements, consider including an option to purchase stock provision in your will. (This can also be accomplished with an inter vivos trust.) This is a method whereby you offer your children a way to buy into the business at your death.

However, there are several things to be careful of, if you choose this option:

1. *Because of changing conditions between now and then, fixing a price for stock now is of no use.* Thus, you need to implement a clear and easy method for how stock prices should be established (i.e., appraisal at death), and keep in mind the prices must reflect fair market value.

Objective 4: Treating Your Children Equitably

2. *Terms must be financially feasible for the ones buying the stock.*

3. *Unless your children have life insurance coverage on you as the parent or owner, this method can place an undue income tax burden on the children, as opposed to a corporate redemption of shares.* They will be purchasing stock with personal after-tax dollars, rather than corporate after-tax dollars, assuming the corporation marginal tax bracket is less than that of the children.

Interplay of Leases

To equalize gifts to your children who are not involved in the business, you may give them gifts of real estate or equipment that are owned outside the business but then leased to the business at a fair market rental rate.

With this strategy, you utilize a long term lease, arranging the lease between both spouses and the company, so when the children inherit the assets, all parties are bound by it.

Close Corporation Status

Your corporation should consider the advantages of electing close corporation status. By unanimous consent, the shareholders may, by agreement (binding upon successor shareholders), regulate the exercise of corporate powers, the management of the business and affairs of the corporation, and relations among the corporation's shareholders.

In the common situation where the father remains the corporation's manager for his lifetime, management authority passes to children active in the business who are ready to take over, while non-active children may receive certain limited voting rights and mandatory dividends. This makes the position of the non-active children similar to that of preferred shareholders. Irrevocable proxies may be given in particular instances.

Additionally, close corporation statutes provide some share transfer restrictions that are similar to many buy-sell agreements.

Limited Partnership

In this arrangement, all children could have equal interests in the company, while also allowing for those children who need to be more involved in management and everyday decisions.

The mother, father and active children would be general partners, and the non-active children could be limited partners. As such, the non-active children would have no decision-making authority and no exposure for creditor claims.

Conversely, as a downside, the general partners *could* face exposure to business creditor claims.

S Corporation Status

Structuring your business as an S corporation allows for a portion of profits to be passed to children not involved in business, without a double tax.

Objective 4: Treating Your Children Equitably

Establish Two Classes of Stock

This strategy involves establishing voting shares and non-voting shares of stock. Voting shares are allocated to the active children, while non-voting shares go to the non-active children. The mother and father can implement this strategy while still living, or they can arrange for it in a will upon their deaths.

This strategy can also be used in S-Corporations, as long as both voting and non-voting classes of stock are common stock with identical liquidation and other economic rights.

Lifetime Sale of the Business

Rather than struggle with the complexities of dividing up business interests, some owners might find it appealing to sell or transfer the family business to their interested children outright. This option comes with several advantages:

1. *Desired ownership is put immediately in place with the active children.*

2. *Future appreciation is diverted from parents, making distribution of assets less complicated.*

3. *Children inactive in the business benefit from cash or promissory notes remaining in the estate.*

4. *Parents may have the option to retire from the business and live on the installment payments from the purchase price, instead of remaining with the business solely to*

receive a salary. (Non-qualified deferral compensation plans should also be considered.)

There is one glaring disadvantage to consider with this option: The parents will likely realize a taxable gain on the sale and subsequently lose the benefit of a stepped-up basis for their stock upon the death of one spouse.

Life Insurance

Many owners prefer to use life insurance as an equalizer, to ensure equitability in their children's inheritance.

Typically, these parents give ownership of the business to their children who are active in the company, while naming their non-active children as beneficiaries in life insurance policies of a value equivalent to a share in the business. The challenge is that it can be difficult to pinpoint the amount of insurance needed at the time of inheritance, but you may base it on the value of the business at the time of the gift.

Finally, remember that no single solution may be right for everyone. In fact, business owners quite often find it necessary to implement several of these strategies in their succession planning.

The goal is to create a structure that works both for the business and the family, treating each of the children equitably. An experienced succession planner can advise you on which options might work best for you.

CHAPTER 7

Objective 5:
Preserving Family Harmony

WITH SUCCESSION PLANNING, AS WITH ESTATE PLANNING, perhaps the greatest potential pitfall is disruption of family unity. Because all interested family members bring expectations and emotional attachments to the table, the planning process may feel something like walking a tightrope–where any decision you make in one person's favor may be taken as an affront by another.

Objective 5: Preserving Family Harmony

For this reason–the fear of causing offense or invoking a feud–many people avoid doing any planning at all.

Of course, as we'll explore in the next chapter, the decision to do nothing is the worst one you could make. It almost guarantees the very feuds you're trying to avoid. Ultimately, you have no control over how others may react, but we'd like to recommend three important steps that may minimize the risk of family conflict, both now and in the future.

Step One: Involve All Affected Parties in the Planning Process

This group includes anyone who has an existing or potential financial interest in the family business, and anyone whom you wish to receive benefit from the company. Obviously, that includes your children, but it may also include extended family members, investors, key employees and others. Get these parties involved in the conversation as early as possible; find out their interest levels, their expectations, etc.

At some point, you'll want to have one or more family meetings to talk about your intentions. During these meetings, allow family members to share their feelings, hammer out any differences, and understand why specific decisions were made.

Once you have everyone on board with the plan, have each interested party commit to the plan in writing. In this manner, you'll have a record of agreement you can rely upon later, if need be.

Step Two: Transfer the Business to the Active Children to the Greatest Extent Possible

This logical strategy will eliminate the majority of arguments for everyone involved. Few people will dispute the notion that the children actively participating in growing the business should stand to gain the most from it.

Feel free to offer minority stakes to inactive children, utilizing some of the strategies we discussed earlier in this book. But recall that, when you set *personal involvement* as the benchmark for ownership stake, you take favoritism out of the equation. No one can accuse you of playing favorites if you hand the business over to those who have invested the most "sweat equity" in the company.

Step Three: Consider Implementing a Buy-Sell Agreement Among the Children

A buy-sell agreement establishes trigger points at which the company, or shares of it, may be bought or sold. This provision gives your children more options down the line and adds some flexibility to your plan. Be sure to include a "stalemate provision," to foster resolutions in the event that conflict arises. (In an upcoming chapter, we'll discuss buy-sell agreements in detail–including the stalemate provision.)

Unfortunately, no plan can guarantee family unity. Sometimes conflict is inevitable, and it has nothing to do with you. However, by being proactive using the steps above, you can reduce the risk

OBJECTIVE 5: PRESERVING FAMILY HARMONY

of conflict by effectively eliminating any legitimate reasons for conflict. In the majority of cases, following these steps will enable your family to come to consensus early and remain in harmony throughout the transition.

CHAPTER 8
Seven Pitfalls that Work Against a Successful Transition

MANY OF US HAVE HEARD SOME VERSION OF THIS STORY: A man tries to hike a steep hill carrying a heavy backpack. He walks until his strength fails, then stops to rest, only to discover he was carrying a backpack full of rocks. Once he empties the backpack, his journey becomes much easier.

Succession planning is weighty enough on its own, but far too often, business owners make this transition much more difficult by carrying their own backpacks full of rocks. Each of the seven pitfalls we're about to discuss can add unnecessary "weight" to your succession plan, possibly even jeopardizing it. Each is also highly preventable. Let's look at these issues one at a time.

Pitfall 1: Having No Plan at All

Perhaps the most obvious of these pitfalls, failure to plan (due largely to procrastination) can put the business in severe jeopardy down the road. Many owners fall into the trap of thinking things will simply work out when the time comes. This act of procrastination makes the company vulnerable to a number of possible disasters. For our purposes, we'll focus on two.

Unintended Structuring

The next generation of the family may be forced into an unintended ownership and/or management scheme. This setup may be disadvantageous both to the business and the management team attempting to run it.

Untimely Death or Disability

Succession planning doesn't just address retirement. It also addresses untimely death and disability, neither of which necessarily waits until retirement age to occur. People tend to underestimate their risks of disability: The Council of Disability Awareness reports that nearly two-thirds of wage earners (64 percent) believe their risk of extended disability is two percent or less, when the actual risk is about 25 percent. These risks go up considerably if the person is overweight or smokes.

The uncertainty created by having no succession plan in place is a threat to the business's longevity in and of itself. Frustrated family members or key employees may leave the business rather than wait for a transition plan to be formulated or enacted. Then, when the time does come, and a transition that is unplanned and unmanaged must be forced upon the business, the effect can be devastating.

Pitfall 2: Failing to Be Objective

When choosing a successor, it is important to make the selection an objective one. Do not choose a carbon copy of yourself, and do not base the decision on sex, birth order, seniority, or loyalty. None of these factors can properly predict the type of person who will best serve the interests of your business once you leave it.

Because a business has a life cycle of its own, a management style that worked at one time may not work in the future. Thus, the decision should be based on the kind of leadership style and management skills the business will need for the years ahead, and the people within the business (family or non-family) who can best do the job. Children already active in the business may not yet be ready to manage it. In such instance, an interim non-family manager may run the company until the children are capable of doing so.

Pitfall 3: Failing to Choose a Successor at All

Sometimes, succession planning involves so many family emotions that a business owner becomes indecisive. If sibling rivalry exists within the family, choosing one child over another to head the business could be interpreted as favoritism, or loving one child over the others. Conversely, if a child decides to leave the business, it could be equated with leaving the family.

An indecisive owner sometimes tries to solve the dilemma with one of the following ill-advised strategies:

- *Letting the next generation decide.* This choice is equivalent to "passing the buck," inviting strife down the road. If it's your business, then it's up to you to decide who should lead it.

- *Setting up shared presidential authority.* This idea is a bad one, too, because it can lead to bickering, organizational confusion and indecision.

Pitfall 4: Failure to Prepare the Successor You Have Chosen.

Family businesses are not usually run like IBM where jobs are filled according to qualification and merit. In the family business, you only need to be a family member to get in, and the roles and responsibilities are often not clearly delineated. Furthermore, there is likely little or no performance accountability where the owner's children or other relatives are concerned.

Of course, we're not suggesting your children shouldn't be involved with your company. However, because family involvement usually occurs without a vetting process, many successors take the helm of the business without proper preparation. Executive development is often sadly neglected, usually consisting of exposing the child to everything in the business, but making him or her responsible for nothing. Parents may not make good mentors for this very reason.

Pitfall 5: Failure to Delegate Responsibility to the Chosen Successor

Tying into the previous pitfall, preparing a successor usually involves delegating some responsibility to him or her before handing over the company. Unfortunately, many owners miss the point of this important step, because they don't realize that *exposure* and *experience* are not the same thing. If you simply show your successor the ins-and-outs of your company without delegating important tasks, you're robbing him or her of vital experience he or she needs to make good decisions.

Successors must have the chance to learn from their mistakes, just like the original owner did. They must have the opportunity to make the decisions they would make, as the one in charge. It's worth repeating:

> *Delegating* **means giving your successor a chance to gain experience, not just exposure.**

Pitfall 6: Failing to Plan for One's Own Retirement

Handing the business over means handing the business over. When it's time for the successor to take over, it's time for you to get out of the way.

Unfortunately, many business owners find it difficult to separate themselves when this time comes. In their minds, no longer working is the same as no longer breathing. They fail to appreciate the fact that they must now retire from their own company and entrust it to someone else.

For the transition to be successful, the business owner must make a plan for his or her retirement. And that includes giving up the right to return to the company. The owner must come to grips with leaving. If the owner does not plan for some place to go with something compelling to do, he or she will likely be back. If the owner comes back or tries to take a lesser role in the business, it will be difficult for him or her to not be involved as before. And that will undermine the successor and open the door for conflict.

Pitfall 7: Failure to Distinguish Between *Ownership* Succession Planning and *Management* Succession Planning

The business owner might have planned for ownership succession of the business through an estate plan. However, this action alone ignores the idea of management succession, which provides a secure future for the business itself. Sometimes business owners aren't those who manage the operations on a day-to-day basis. In that case, it's natural to differentiate between owner and management succession. However, for more involved owners, if you transfer ownership to a successor without transferring management control as well, then you risk making your successor little more than a figurehead.

If the successor is to run the business, you must make specific decisions regarding voting control. Will you transfer control directly to the successor? If other stockholders are involved, is a voting trust appropriate? A succession planner can advise you on the best way to structure management succession for your company.

CHAPTER 9
What a Good Succession Planner Will Do
A Checklist So Owners Know They Are Being Well Taken Care Of

BY THIS POINT IN THE BOOK, YOU UNDERSTAND the importance of succession planning: It is essential to ensure the future of your business and the well-being of your family. That said, a good succession *plan* emerges with the help of a good succession *planner*. How can you tell if your planner is doing a good job for you? How can you be sure everything is being covered effectively?

What a Good Succession Planner Will Do

To pull back the curtain a bit on the succession planning process, so you can track with your planner and make sure you're not missing any important points, we've created the comprehensive checklist below. If some of the terminology on this list seems foreign to you, don't fret. Just ask your planner. (If you're working with a knowledgeable planner that person should be able to explain it without a problem.)

The Overall Planning Process

A good succession planner will do the following:

- *Encourage clients to start planning as early as possible.* A good succession planner will encourage you to start thinking about succession in your 40s and 50s, rather than 70s or 80s (although later is better than never).

- *Gather information about the business and the client's objectives.* The planner will use this to establish reasonable goals for passing the business to the next generation.

- *Determine the appropriate method to achieve the client's goals.*

- *Make recommendations, provide a methodology for implementing the recommendations, and actually walk the client through the implementation process.* Good succession planners don't just tell you what to do, they guide you step-by-step.

- *Incorporate estate tax savings strategies with the business in mind.* Even though planning for estate tax savings is important, the planner must understand family and business dynamics, as well. Without these, the succession plan may be destroyed.

The Steps of Succession Planning

Here's what the actual planning process should look like, from the perspective of what the planner needs to accomplish.

- *Review historical and pro forma financial statements and all existing pertinent legal documents.* This includes, potentially among other documents, wills, trust agreements, existing shareholders and buy-sell agreements, employment contracts, leases, incorporation papers, partnership agreements, S-Corporation elections, prenuptial agreements and deferred compensation arrangements.

- *Review the existing estate structure, including how many heirs there are and who they are.* In particular, the planner is looking for the best options and structures to suit your needs. Leaving the business to too many heirs or a non-qualifying trust, for example, could result in the loss of an S-Corporation election.

- *Translate financial statements to current fair market value.*

- *Analyze business debt, capital structure, and cash flows.* This includes:
  - Reviewing accounts receivable, inventory, and fixed assets to determine if there is sufficient collateral for a leveraged buyout and sufficient cash flow to amortize new debt.
  - Determining the impact the principal owner's death would have on current customers.
- *Identify key management personnel and determine how the business will operate in the owner's absence.* This step includes devising an incentive plan to retain key employees. Incentive methods may include:
  - Phantom stock arrangement
  - Stock appreciation rights plans
  - Accrued bonus plan based on a percentage of the profits.
- *Determine the owner's desires to maintain jobs for family members and have the business succession be transferred to family members.* This includes not only deciding which of the active family members will stay, but also deciding which of the non-productive family members should be encouraged to stay home or work outside the business. Methods to implement this have been previously discussed.

- *Identify potential purchasers of the business, if family succession is not a requirement and the owner desires to possibly sell the business.* The list could include:
  - Existing management
  - Other family members
  - A competitor or customer
  - An LBO fund
  - Employees using a stock option plan (ESOP)
- *Determine the current market value of the business.* Obtain an appraisal from a reputable firm, or use the following eight factors from Revenue Ruling 59-60:
  - The nature and history of the business
  - The economic outlook and condition of the industry
  - The book value and financial condition of the business
  - The earning capacity of the business
  - The dividend-paying capacity of the business
  - The value of any goodwill or other intangibles
  - The degree of control represented by the size of the block of stock interest
  - The value of similar stocks traded on open markets
- *Project the size of the taxable estate at the time of death, as well as estate and inheritance tax liabilities.* The planner should help you plan for enough liquidity in your estate to cover all expected business and personal

needs. Life insurance may be a good option for liquidity or planning purposes.

- *Determine the owner's income needs after retirement/succession and how these will be met.* Options to meet this goal may include:
  - Existing qualified benefit plans (e.g., profit sharing, pension)
  - Non-qualified deferred compensation plans
  - A stream of income derived from the succession plan (e.g., installment sale of stock, consulting arrangement or non-compete agreement). **NOTE:** For this option, the planner should review the income tax consequences and effect on loss of Social Security benefits

Additional Considerations

Throughout the planning process, a good succession planner will counsel you with the following in mind:

- *Succession planning is a process, not an event.* As time passes and situations change or the company evolves, changes may have to be made.

- *Communication is key.* The owner should communicate the plan to his or her family members and key employees and involve them in the succession planning process, both for the good of the business and the unity of the family.

- ***The owner's needs and wants should dictate the plan—not taxes.*** A good planner will keep tax avoidance in mind when counseling on a plan, but the succession plan must first fulfill the owner's and family's needs and those of the business. Then the proper structure for the succession plan can be determined.

CHAPTER 10
Structuring Buy-Sell Agreements

WHEN A FAMILY BUSINESS HAS MULTIPLE OWNERS, succession planning becomes a bit more complicated. If you have a part ownership stake in a business, either with other family members or with non-family members, what happens to your part of the company when you pass on or are somehow disabled? What if your share goes to a surviving spouse or child who has little interest in the company? How would such a situation affect the other owners? Appointing a successor or transferring your shares gets understandably tricky when you have other voting members to consider, all with their own interests to protect.

In situations like these, succession planners will usually recommend setting up a buy-sell agreement to protect the interests of surviving owners and family members. This agreement designates certain events (e.g., death or disability of an owner) as "triggering events" that either a) require surviving owners to purchase the interest of the departing owner; or b) provide remaining owners the option to buy the owner's interest. Buy-sell agreements work with any type of multi-owner business, but they can be especially effective for corporations with numerous stockholders.

***Hand in hand with buy-sell agreements, you need to arrange a payment method for purchasing the departed owner's shares when a triggering event occurs. Many businesses accomplish this by means of a life insurance policy.

Planners recommend buy-sell agreements for three basic purposes:

- To provide a method that assures ownership and control of the corporation will stay in the hands of the remaining owners upon certain events;
- To provide a ready market for selling a stockholder's shares; and
- To provide for a source of liquidity for the estate of a deceased stockholder.

Types of Buy-Sell Agreements

Buy-sell agreements generally fall into one of three categories:

- *The redemption agreement:* Under this agreement, the *corporation* is the potential buyer and is either obligated or has the option to buy at the time of a triggering event.

- *The cross-purchase agreement:* In this case, *company stockholders themselves* are the potential buyers and are obligated or have the option to buy after a triggering event.

- *The hybrid agreement:* This structure combines features of a redemption agreement and cross purchase agreement. In this case, the corporation has the primary obligation or option to buy out the stockholder's shares, while a secondary obligation or option exists for the remaining stockholders. (Even though cross-purchase agreements may be a better way, many clients prefer the redemption structure. Hybrid agreements supply the flexibility needed to go either way.)

Must-Haves for Any Buy-Sell Agreement

Regardless of which structure you decide is best, your buy-sell agreement should include crucial elements to eliminate all possible ambiguity. Let's go over these elements briefly.

Structuring Buy-Sell Agreements

Voluntary and Involuntary Transfers

You need to specify that both voluntary and involuntary transfers are covered by the agreement. And include in the document a clear definition of what is meant by a "transfer." Here's a good example:

> *No stockholder shall sell, give, assign, transfer, or in any manner dispose of or encumber or permit to be sold, assigned, encumbered, attached, or otherwise disposed of or transferred in any manner, either voluntarily or by operation of law (all hereinafter collectively referred to as "transfer") ....*

You also need to specify what is not meant to be a "transfer." For example, the term "transfer" may not include a statutory merger transaction. "Transfer" may also not include assignments to a Revocable Trust of the stockholder during the stockholder's lifetime, if the stockholder is the sole trustee. However, make sure this assignment does not pose a problem with any S corporation election.

Triggering Events

Your agreement needs to identify specific triggering events that will enact the transfer. Among the most common types of triggering events are:

- The death of the stockholder
- The termination of the employee/stockholder for any reason
- The "total disability" of the employee/stockholder

For the last point, you need to include a definition of "total disability." For example:

The disabled shareholder's attending physician shall certify that—as a result of any medically determinable physical or mental impairment, sickness or bodily injury requiring care and treatment by a physician—the disabled stockholder lacks the skills or abilities he or she previously possessed, such that the stockholder is unable to perform any substantial and material part of his or her ordinary duties with regularity over a significant period of time.

Marital Impact

Marriages and divorces can have an unintended impact on ownership stakes in a business, causing what we call "marital property exposure"— that is, the situation in which a spouse or ex-spouse has claim to company shares as a result of marriage to the stockholder. This situation may greatly complicate the transfer of ownership after a triggering event. For this reason, your buy-sell agreement should provide for any possible marital property impact in the event of exposure.

A marital property exposure may be created by either the death of a stockholder's spouse or a divorce, dissolution or legal separation. Exposure is *specifically* created when three conditions come into existence:

- The marriage has ended by divorce, dissolution or legal separation;

Structuring Buy-Sell Agreements

- The spouse has a marital property interest in the stockholder's shares; and

- The stockholder does not receive the spouse's interest through the property settlement agreement.

To resolve these types of issues, your buy-sell agreement should identify in whom the right to buy the now-deceased spouse's marital property shares is vested. It should also identify in whom the right to buy the *former* spouse's marital property shares is vested.

Obligation to Purchase/Sell

For each triggering event listed, your agreement must spell out who has the option or obligation to purchase, as well as who has the obligation to sell. These terms may be different for each type of triggering event, or they may be the same for all. Just make sure the terms are clear in every case.

Contract Purchase Price

Your agreement should include a formula either establishing a contract price or detailing a method of appraisal to obtain a purchase price for shares being sold.

Under the old rules (for agreements in place on or before October 8, 1990 and which are not substantially modified after that date), for the price established in the buy-sell agreement to be binding for purposes of death, it must generally comply with the following:

- It must be a bona fide business arrangement.

- It must not be a device to transfer property to members of the decedent's family for less than full and adequate consideration in money or money's worth.

- The price must be determinable under the terms of the agreement.

- The owner of the property and his estate must be obligated to sell, and the company or other owners must agree to buy, at the contract price. Some agreements require the prospective buyer to purchase the property, but this provision is not mandatory; possession of an option is sufficient.

- The obligation to sell at the contract price must be binding both during life and after death.

For buy-sell agreements enacted after October 8, 1990—or those enacted prior to that date which have been substantially modified—Chapter 14 of the Revenue Reconciliation Act of 1990 adds another factor which must be met, in order for the price to be binding in the event of the death of any of the parties to the agreement. That additional factor is that the terms "must be comparable to similar arrangements entered into by persons in an arm's length transaction."

This new test applies to agreements entered into by unrelated parties, as well as family related agreements. This last test makes it more questionable as to whether or not the Internal Revenue Service will use the price established in the buy-sell agreement as binding in the event of the death of a stockholder for estate tax purposes. The only way to be sure of the price is to obtain an independent appraisal at death to determine value.

Means of Funding

Your agreement should describe a means of funding the purchase(s) when a triggering event occurs. This funding may occur by a number of methods:

- *Life insurance.* One of the most common payment strategies, life insurance is written on the life of each stockholder. The death benefit provides the money needed to purchase the stock shares. Whole life insurance is preferred over term insurance because the premiums are stable, and because the cash surrender value can be borrowed or used in later years to help fund a buyout during the stockholder's lifetime.

- *Disability insurance.*

- *Unsecured promissory notes.* These notes are used in many instances for any purchase of stock from an estate that is not covered by insurance, and more often for purchases of stock from a stockholder who has become disabled or has terminated his employment with the company.

- *Funds accumulated by the buyer.*

- *A stockholder trust.* The stockholders form the trust, contribute money for insurance policies, and are paid by the trustee when the money is needed. This method is most often used in cross purchase arrangements with many stockholders.

S Corporation Election

Provide protection for S corporation election, if any. Do so by requiring that no transfer will be made without the prior written consent of all stockholders, to any corporation, partnership, trust or any other transferee, if effects of the transfer will cause the S corporation election to be lost or revoked. This language also supports the reasonableness of the buy-sell agreement's transfer restrictions.

Stock Transfer Restrictions

Provide for the stock certificates to be clearly marked with a notice that stock transfer restrictions are in effect. Language such as this is clear:

> *Any sale, assignment, transfer, pledge or other disposition of the shares of stock represented by this certificate is restricted by and subject to the terms of a stock restriction and purchase agreement dated as of _____, 20____, and may be sold or otherwise transferred only upon proof of compliance therewith. By acceptance of this certificate, the holder hereof agrees to be bound by the terms of that agreement.*

Failure to Perform

The buy-sell agreement should include a statement that if there is a failure to perform by a party or by the decedent's personal representative, all parties agree it is impossible to measure in money the damages that will accrue. Therefore, specific performance is the only remedy that will suffice.

Voting Trust Option

This provision states that shares may be transferred to a voting trust. The language should make clear that the shares and voting trust certificate, if any, are still subject to the buy-sell agreement. It should also state that, regardless of transfer, the stockholder remains the holder of the corporation stock for purposes of the buy-sell agreement.

Invalid Transfers

Included in the language should be a provision that any transfer or attempted transfer in violation of the agreement is null and void, and therefore ineffective.

Voting Directives

The agreement should provide voting directives for when the corporation is required to act regarding a stockholder option or offer. Specifically:

- The said stockholder must vote or refrain from voting as directed by the majority stockholder.
- If the said stockholder is a director, he or she must vote or refrain from voting as directed by the majority of the remaining stockholders.

- The said stockholder must attend all stockholder or board of directors' meetings when his presence is needed for a quorum.

- If said stockholder fails, he or she waives any objection and approves all action taken.

Adherence to the Agreement

Include a provision in the agreement that shares transferred in compliance with the agreement are still subject to the agreement, and that all purchasers/transferees are deemed to have accepted and consented to be bound by the agreement.

Amending the Agreement

To keep the buy-sell agreement relevant over time, make sure it provides the ability to amend the agreement by a majority vote of shareholders if they so desire, provided such change will not be to the detriment of anyone who has previously had his stock purchased by the company. This allows the agreement to be more flexible in the event the facts change.

Redemption Versus Cross-Purchase Agreements

You'll recall from earlier in our discussion that the three types of buy-sell agreements are *redemption agreements, cross-purchase agreements* and *hybrid agreements* (which combine characteristics of the first two). Let's now explore the first two types in a bit more detail, because even though redemption and cross-purpose agreements have the same purpose, there are fundamental differences between them.

Structuring Buy-Sell Agreements

Redemption Agreements

In redemption agreements, the targeted buyer is the corporation itself, not the individual stockholders. These agreements are easier to administer and monitor because everything centers around the corporation. When funded by insurance, the policies are owned by the corporation, the premiums are paid by the corporation, and the corporation is the beneficiary. When a triggering event occurs, the corporation uses the money to buy the shares.

When using insurance to fund redemption agreement triggers, there is only one policy for each of the stockholders. Therefore, if there are five stockholders, there will be only five policies.

Cross-Purchase Agreements

Cross-purchase agreements are a bit more complicated than redemption agreements because the targeted buyers are the other stockholders, instead of the corporation. When funded by insurance, the policies are each owned by the individual stockholders, the premiums are paid by the individual stockholders, and the beneficiaries are the individual stockholders. The corporation may pay the premiums on these policies, but if it does, the amount may be considered a distribution of dividends to the stockholder, which could result in tax consequences.

Additionally, because each stockholder holds a policy on the life of each of the other stockholders in a cross-purchase agreement, if there are five stockholders, there could be 20 policies. (However, this can be avoided by the use of a shareholder trust, partnerships or S corporation, as we will discuss later.)

Business Succession Planning

Despite its complexities, in recent corporate buy-sell planning, the cross-purchase method has been heavily favored over redemption agreements for a variety of reasons:

- Premium dollars are taxed at the 21 percent corporate tax rate (and for all personal service corporation income) versus a 37 percent bracket for individuals.

- The surviving shareholders in a cross-purchase plan enjoy an increase in basis equal to the price of the stock purchased by each. (The C Corporation redemption results in no basis increase.)

- In a family-owned situation, the cross purchase avoids any IRC § 318 attribution problems which can result in dividend (ordinary income) treatment to the estate in a redemption.

- Because of the transfer for value rule, it is easy to switch from a cross-purchase agreement to a redemption agreement, if desired. (It can be more difficult to go the other way around.)

- A cross-purchase agreement avoids any reduction in the corporation's net worth and avoids any leveraging with debt on the corporation's balance sheet, as would occur with a stock redemption.

One potential challenge for cross-purchase agreements is that deductibility of interest for the shareholder/purchaser may be a problem when a promissory note is given during a lifetime purchase if the corporation is a C Corporation for tax purposes. The company may have to make an S corporation election prior to the individual stockholder purchasing the stock, in order to deduct any interest expense on payments made by such shareholder for the purchase of stock.

Tax Considerations for Redemption and Cross-Purchase Agreements

Both redemption and cross-purchase agreements offer attractive features, but with those features come tax considerations and consequences. Let's discuss some of those considerations now.

Redemption Agreements: Capital Gains or Dividends

A redemption is a repurchase by a corporation of its own stock. As such, it is a distribution subject to the rules of §§ 301 and 316, which means money received by the stockholder may be considered a dividend. Whether the redemption amount is treated as a dividend or a capital gain, the impact is still significant to the stockholder.

When the redemption is treated as a dividend: The amount of the distribution that is treated as a dividend is taxable to the stockholder at a maximum rate of 15 percent. However, as a sale or exchange, the stockholder is entitled to offset his stock basis against the amount received, and only the excess is taxable as capital gains at a top rate of 15 percent if the stock had been owned for more than 12 months. Since the death of the stockholder may be the triggering event, an added tax benefit is incurred when the basis in the stock is adjusted to fair market value per § 1014. This results in little, if any, capital gain being recognized.

When the redemption is treated as capital gain: There are several provisions in the Internal Revenue Code allowing redemption proceeds to receive capital gains treatment:

- Redemption of all the stockholder's shares in the corporation is a complete redemption and is treated as a sale or exchange of stock. (I.R.C. § 302(b)(3)) Family and entity attribution (trust, partnership and corporation) must be carefully considered before using a redemption agreement (§ 318). Even with careful planning, if a redemption occurs and a remaining stockholder's shares are attributed to a selling stockholder, the selling stockholder may end up with the full purchase price for his shares being taxed as a dividend.

- Redemptions that are substantially disproportionate are treated as sales. (I.R.C. § 302(b)(2)) To be "substantially disproportionate," the redemption must meet a two-part test:
  - The redeeming shareholder must own less than 50 percent of the voting power of all classes of voting stock following the redemption; and
  - The redeeming shareholder after the redemption must own less than 80 percent of the common stock and voting stock owned before the redemption.

For family owned corporations, the family attribution rule contained in § 318 may prevent the redeeming shareholder from meeting the 20 percent reduction in interest test.

- "A redemption that is a partial liquidation of the corporation is treated as a sale." (I.R.C. § 302(b)(4)) This provision does stipulate the redeeming stockholder cannot be a corporation. There are also further exceptions in §§ 302 and 303 to the distribution rules of § 301.

Redemption Agreements: Imputed Interest on Installments Sales

In instances where liquidity is not a serious concern to the seller, all or a portion of the redemption proceeds may be paid by the corporation in installments with interest. The interest rate charged must be adequate in order not to trigger the imputed rules under I.R.C. § 1274. Under this rule, if the interest rate is not equal to or greater than the applicable federal rate, determined pursuant to the rules of that section, the amount of interest for income and deduction purposes is recomputed. The overall effect is that a portion of the stated principal amount is converted into interest, which increases the taxpayer's taxable income.

Cross Purchase Agreements: Stockholder Policies Owned by Shareholder Trusts, Partnerships or Sub S-Corporations

When the stockholders number more than a few, the number of insurance policies needed increases dramatically, resulting in greater expense to the stockholders. All policies must be monitored so they are kept in force. When a triggering event occurs, transferring the existing policies may present a challenge.

To simplify this process, the stockholders can form an insurance trust, a partnership or an S corporation, which will own the individual policies. For a trust, the insurance proceeds are distributed to each of the remaining stockholders at the time of death. For the S corporation or partnership, such entity is the party to the agreement and is obligated, or has an option, to purchase stock when a triggering event occurs. Additionally, the S corporation or partnership should have a business purpose other than strictly to own life insurance.

Other Tax Effects of Buy-Sell Agreements

Before we leave this discussion, we need to mention a few additional tax considerations of either redemption or cross-purchase agreements, as follows.

Redemption Agreements: Tax Impact on Buyer Corporation and Other Stockholders

Regardless of whether the distribution to the stockholders is treated as a dividend (under I.R.C. § 301) or as a sale (under I.R.C. §§ 302 or 303), if the redemption proceeds are paid in cash, the corporation will recognize neither gain nor loss. However, if the corporation uses appreciated property to redeem the stock, this action is recognized as a gain.

Generally, a stock redemption does not affect the other stockholders; however, if the other stockholders had a primary and unconditional obligation to purchase the stock, the purchase is treated as a constructive dividend to those stockholders. (Rev. Rul. 69 608, 1969 2 C.B. 42; *Pulliam v. Commissioner*, 48 T.C.M. 1019, T.C. Memo 1984 470; *Jacobs v. Commissioner*, 41 T.C.M. 951, T.C. Memo 1981 81, aff'd, 698 F.2d 850 (6th Cir. 1983)). To avoid this occurrence, give the stockholders the option to purchase, and let the corporation's purchase rights arise only when the stockholders fail to exercise their option.

Cross-Purchase Agreements: Tax Impact on Stockholders

Upon a triggering event, the selling stockholders will have a capital gain or loss. However, if the death of the stockholder is the major triggering event, I.R.C. § 1014 will adjust the stockholder's basis to fair market value and therefore minimize, or even negate, any capital gains.

In addition, purchasing stockholders will use cost as their tax basis for their newly purchased shares with a new holding period. This is an advantage over a redemption of stock where the remaining shareholders' ownership percentages may increase, but their tax basis for their shares does not increase because they are not purchasing any shares.

Thirdly, interest payments made by purchasing stockholders through an installment sale are generally deductible under I.R.C. § 163(a). That said, the amount of investment interest deductible by a non-corporate taxpayer is limited to the amount of the taxpayer's net investment income. (I.R.C. § 163(d)).

Recent Law Changes: Using Life Insurance as an Investment Vehicle

There are added income tax benefits to using whole life insurance as a funding vehicle by reinvesting the investment component in more insurance. However, recent enactments in the law, such as § 7702 and § 7702(A), have restricted the use of life insurance as an investment (i.e., what was known as universal life), making this benefit less accessible.

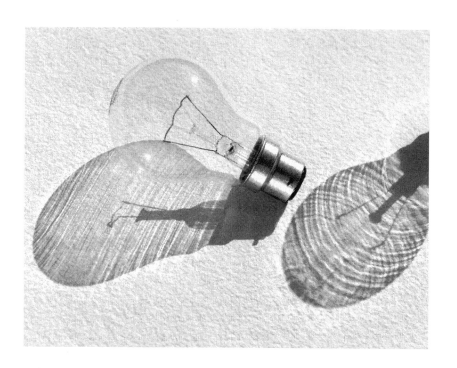

CHAPTER 11
The Key Employee Agreement

IF YOU HAVE ONE OR MORE KEY EMPLOYEES whom you hope remain with your company after you leave, you'll need a well-structured key employee agreement to make sure everyone's interests are protected, through the transition and beyond. As previously discussed, a "key employee" is a person (generally non-family) who has high decision-making authority and/or an ownership stake in your business.

The Key Employee Agreement

When to Use a Key Employee Agreement

We highly recommend owners implement a key employee agreement, if one or more of the following scenarios apply:

- *The owner has no apparent successor to the business within the family.* For example, if the children are all minors or not in any way involved with the business.

- *The owner desires to sell the business in later years.*

- *The owner realizes that the value of the business may be tied dramatically to his/her presence, or to the presence of key employees.* If the owner dies, how likely is it that the key employee would leave the company or even start a competing company, possibly taking clients with him or her? A key employee agreement could avert this problem. (A non-compete agreement may also help.)

- *One or more key employees may be the likely future owners of the business, but they do not have the opportunity or financial ability to purchase the business during the owner's lifetime.*

Objectives of the Key Employee Agreement

An owner may desire to implement a key employee agreement to accomplish any or all of the following goals:

- *Freedom during the owner's lifetime (without any restrictions) to either sell his/her stock in the business or gift said stock to family members who may later become active in the business.*

- *Securing a purchaser for the business in the event of the owner's premature death, and therefore increasing liquidity for the estate.*

- *Obtaining fair market value for the business, and not a value which is depreciated by the owner's premature death.*

- *Providing an incentive for key employees to remain with the business.* The key employees have the security of knowing that, if the owner dies prematurely, they will succeed to ownership of the company. If the agreement terminates for any reason, the key employees will receive a return of the premiums paid, plus a fair rate of interest (six percent), in return for the transfer of the life insurance on the owner's life to either owner or the company.

- *Short-term protection for the business in the event of untimely death.* For example, the owner may want to have the protection of a key employee purchase of owner's stock in the event of a premature death, but, once the children become adults in their 20s or 30s, the owner may want the option of changing the succession plan from a transfer to key employees to a transfer to the owner's next generation.

The Key Employee Agreement

Terms of the Key Employee Agreement

A good key employment agreement must have particular concepts, terms and essential considerations in place. Let's go over these now.

Parties to the Agreement

The parties to the agreement are: the owner; the company; and identified key employees (or an entity formed by them) who wish to participate in the potential buy out of the capital stock of the company from the owner in the event of his or her death.

General Concepts

Purchasing shares: In the event of the death of the owner prior to selling the business to some other third party (or transferring the business to the owner's adult children), the key employees who are parties to the agreement will purchase a portion of the shares of the company owned by the estate of the owner for an agreed upon price, paying for such shares in full or in part with life insurance which such participants have purchased on the owner's life.

The remainder of the shares would be purchased by the company, also at an agreed-upon price, but with payment by the corporation delivering to the estate a promissory note for the balance of the purchase price. The company could also purchase life insurance on the owner's life and purchase his or her shares of stock for cash; however, then the owner would be in fact indirectly paying for the insurance premiums to redeem his or her own shares, and the insurance owned by the company would increase the value of the company in the owner's estate in the event of his or her death.

Payment of insurance premiums: Key employees would pay the premiums on the life insurance out of their own funds (whether assets or compensation) without any assistance from the owner, or they may borrow a portion of such premiums from the company.

If the owner sells the company: In the event the owner sells the company during his or her lifetime to some other third party, the owner would repurchase the life insurance on his or her life from the key employees at a cost equal to their premiums paid (net of any loans on such policies), plus a six percent per annum return of investment for their involvement in the agreement.

Fair market value: The owner and the key employees must agree annually on a fair market value for such shares, and if they cannot agree on such value, the agreement will terminate. The owner may terminate the agreement at any time, but if so, he or she must repurchase the insurance from the key employees at the agreed-upon price.

Termination: In the event the owner wishes to terminate the agreement, he or she may be able to purchase life insurance on his or her life from the key employees in later years, when he or she may not be insurable.

This structure puts the owner in a win/win situation: He/she can sell the stock at any time to a third party or gift it as he or she so desires, but, in the event of death, the owner's shares

The Key Employee Agreement

will be purchased by key employees and the corporation for a fair arm's length price, giving the owner's estate the liquidity it may require. In addition, the continuation of the business (and jobs for its loyal employees) will not be jeopardized by the owner's premature death.

Let's now look at the terms of the agreement in more detail.

Specific Terms

- *The key employees will purchase life insurance on the owner in an amount as agreed upon to fund the purchase of their portion of the shares of capital stock owned by the owner in the company.* The funds used for the purchase of life insurance will be those of the key employees (or funds borrowed in part from the company), as this will be in effect an investment/savings program for them whereby they will either end up purchasing the stock of the company or will have the life insurance repurchased by the owner or the company for their cost, plus a six percent per annum return on investment.

- *If any key employee wishes to withdraw from the agreement at any time, he or she may do so, at which point either the company or the owner will repurchase that portion of the life insurance owned by said key employee.* The other key employees may not purchase such life insurance from any withdrawing key employee, since the transfer for value rules may impose negative tax effects. The owner or the company could repurchase such insurance, or the key employees could form an entity (e.g., an S corporation, partnership or trust) to purchase the insurance on the owner's life; such entity would be the party to the agreement and would have the obligation of purchasing a portion of the stock from the owner's estate in the event of his or her premature death. In the event the key employees form an entity to purchase the insurance, no change in ownership of the life insurance occurs when a key employee wishes to withdraw; he or she merely sells his or her interest in the entity. However, there would have to be funds in the entity (formed by key employees) available to repurchase a terminating key employee's interest in such entity.

- *Unlike a buy-sell agreement in which the owner may be restricted from transferring his or her shares, the key employee agreement permits the owner to sell or gift his or her stock at any time to any third parties (or family members) without any restrictions on transfer.*

- *In the event the owner does sell or gift his or her stock, the owner or the corporation must repurchase the life insurance policies from the key employees for their original cost (net of policy loans), plus a six percent per annum return on investment.*

- *Upon the owner's death, the key employees (or an entity formed by them) would collect the life insurance proceeds*

The Key Employee Agreement

payable upon the death of an owner. The key employees would be required to repurchase from the owner's estate that portion of the stock which is agreed upon and would pay for such stock with the insurance proceeds. In the event of a shortfall, a promissory note would be given for the difference. In the event of an excess amount of insurance, the key employees would be able to retain such amount or may be required to reinvest such amount in the company. The corporation would purchase the remaining shares at the agreed upon value for a promissory note, possibly with the requirement that any excess insurance funds received by the key employees would be contributed to the corporation by them to reduce the amount of such note. The promissory note owed by the corporation (and guaranteed by the key employees) may be secured by a pledge of the stock being purchased by the key employees, or may be secured by a pledge of certain assets of the company (i.e., a mortgage on real estate; a security interest in equipment).

- *The value of the company stock should be fixed at least annually, possibly with some formula for increases in the value during each year based on the profits or reductions in the value based on the losses since the last fixed value.* In the event the parties cannot agree upon the value, this could be grounds for terminating the agreement, with the resulting repurchase of life insurance by the owner or the company from the key employees. Another consideration for valuing the company (based on the new valuation rules) may be the use of a periodic appraisal or an appraisal at death; however, if only appraised at death, the certainty of the amount of purchase price is not known prior to death.

- *The agreement terminates upon the occurrence of one of the following events:*
  - Termination of the agreement by the owner with prior written notice required;
  - Written agreement of all key employees who are parties to the agreement;
  - The sale or transfer by the owner during his or her lifetime of a majority of the stock in the company to a third party or family member who will succeed the owner in running the company; or
  - The bankruptcy, receivership dissolution or liquidation of the company.

In the event of termination of the agreement prior to the owner's death and purchase of his or her stock, the owner or company must repurchase from the key employees, and the key employees must sell to the owner or company, the insurance policies on the owner's life for the price as discussed.

The Key Employee Agreement

Other Provisions

- A restrictive endorsement should be put on the owner's stock certificates referring to the terms of the key employee agreement.

- The remedy of specific performance should be provided since damages may be inadequate.

- The Board of Directors should issue corporate approval authorizing the company to enter into the agreement.

- There should be an agreement and consent of the key employees' spouses whereby each spouse gifts to the respective key employee as individual property all of spouse's present and future marital property interests in the life insurance owned by the key employee on the owner's life, in addition to a consent by each spouse of a key employee to the key employee entering into the terms of the agreement.

- In addition, as an incentive for allowing the opportunity to key employees to enter into this agreement whereby they may become the owners of the company, the owner may require each key employee to sign a Non-Compete Agreement limiting such person from competing with the company for a period of time in the event he or she terminates employment with the company.

Final Thoughts Regarding the Key Employee Agreement

The key employee agreement is not meant for the typical situation in which a number of owners are attempting to keep the management and control of the business among them. However, this agreement can be very advantageous if a) there is one owner having no logical successor; b) the owner may wish to sell the company prior to death, or transfer it to family members when they become adults; or c) the owner believes the future ownership of the company best resides in a group of key employees.

In the situations mentioned above, a key employee agreement can guarantee liquidity in the event of the owner's premature death, by providing for the mandatory purchase of his or her stock at fair market value by the key employees and company, yet, at the same time, it allows the owner the freedom to sell or transfer his or her stock at any time to an outside third party, family member or company without any restriction.

Epilogue

AS WE CONCLUDE OUR DISCUSSION, let's return to something we said back in the introduction of this book. As owner of a family business, you are part of one of the most significant economic sectors in the United States. More than half of the American workforce works at businesses just like yours. You are also part are the largest job-creating machine in America, as family-owned companies account for nearly 80 percent of all new jobs created.

By this point, you not only understand the importance of succession planning, but you also have a good starting point for implementing it in your own business. Of course, the primary

Epilogue

goal in succession planning is to secure your family's future. However, remember that yours isn't the only family affected.

If your business fails due to improper planning, your children's future affected, but so arethe futures of every employee who works for your company. By taking steps to take your company into the next generation, you're potentially benefitting every member of your team, their families and their descendants after them. And it's not overstating it to say that you're playing a key role in securing the economy of our nation, too.

As you now know, succession planning is not an easy task, and it is a process, not an event. However, by starting early and planning smartly, you can eventually retire, knowing your company is left in good hands.

We wish you well in your endeavors.

About Our Law Firm

What you might want to know about us...

The attorneys at O'Neil, Cannon, Hollman, DeJong & Laing S.C. focus on meeting the many needs of businesses and their owners. Our experienced attorneys work with businesses and their owners at all stages of the business life cycle, helping them start, grow, and transition their businesses from one generation to the next. We also assist business owners with their personal legal needs including tax and estate planning, family law, and litigation—including personal injury litigation. Our firm is divided into six practice groups, each focusing on providing their clients with the most effective legal representation possible. Our teams regularly collaborate to ensure that our clients' needs are met with exceptional legal service.

The firm's practice groups include:

- Litigation, including business litigation, class action litigation, appellate services, arbitration/mediation, plaintiff's personal injury litigation, and family law.

- Business Law, including commercial loan

representation, bankruptcy, employment law, employee benefits and ERISA, franchise/dealership law, and intellectual property.

- Banking & Creditors' Rights, including drafting and negotiating loan agreements and collateral documents in real estate, asset-based and non-recourse financing transactions.

- Employment Law, including providing general employment counsel for employers, drafting and reviewing employment agreements, policies and handbooks, wage and hour compliance, ADA and FMLA compliance, union issues, OSHA, and employment litigation.

- Tax & Succession Planning, including business succession planning, estate planning, tax advice and planning, and tax litigation.

- Real Estate & Construction, including real estate development and land use law, as well as construction law.

Because we know that businesses and their owners rely on attorneys during some of the most fulfilling—and frightening—times in their lives, we combine the experience and proficiency level of a large firm with the personal approach and level of service found at a local law firm.

Our firm is rated AV, the highest rating possible for legal knowledge and ethics, by the prestigious Martindale—Hubbell Law Directory, and has been named a Best Law Firm by U.S. News and World Report for many years. Many of our lawyers are named year-after-year to the list of Wisconsin Super Lawyers and as Best Lawyers, rankings based on rigorous peer review.

Learn more about us at **www.wilaw.com**.

O'NEIL CANNON HOLLMAN DEJONG & LAING s.c.

Wisconsin's Premier Lawyers & Litigators

111 E Wisconsin Ave.
Milwaukee, WI 53202
414.276.5000

Port Washington
1329 West Grand Ave., Suite 200
Port Washington, Wisconsin 53074
262.284.3407

Green Bay
716 Pine Street
Green Bay, Wisconsin 54301
920.569.1540

www.wilaw.com

Disclaimer

You understand that this book is not intended as a substitution for a consultation with an attorney.

Requesting this book or viewing information in it does not create an attorney-client relationship with the Law Offices of O'Neil, Cannon, Hollman, DeJong & Laing S.C. (Hereafter "O'NEIL, ET AL.") or any of its attorneys. To obtain legal advice, please engage the services of O'NEIL, ET AL. or another law firm of your choice. To discuss engaging O'NEIL, ET AL. to help you with your matter, please contact the firm.

THE LAW OFFICES OF O'NEIL, CANNON, HOLLMAN, DEJONG & LAING S.C. IS PROVIDING THIS BOOK THE ART, SCIENCE AND LAW OF BUSINESS SUCCESSION (HEREAFTER REFERRED TO AS "BOOK") AND ITS CONTENTS ON AN "AS IS" BASIS AND MAKES NO REPRESENTATIONS OR WARRANTIES OF ANY KIND WITH RESPECT TO THIS BOOK OR ITS CONTENTS. THE LAW OFFICES OF O'NEIL, ET AL. DISCLAIM ALL SUCH REPRESENTATIONS AND WARRANTIES, INCLUDING FOR EXAMPLE WARRANTIES OF MERCHANTABILITY AND FITNESS FOR A PARTICULAR PURPOSE. IN ADDITION, THE LAW OFFICES OF O'NEIL, ET AL. DO NOT REPRESENT OR WARRANT THAT THE INFORMATION ACCESSIBLE VIA THIS BOOK IS ACCURATE, COMPLETE OR CURRENT.

The book is provided for information purposes only, and relevant laws frequently change. Except as specifically stated in this book, neither The Law Offices of O'Neil, Cannon, Hollman, DeJong & Laing S.C., nor any authors, contributors or other representatives will be liable for damages arising out of or in connection with the use of this book. This is a comprehensive limitation of liability that applies to all damages of any kind, including (without limitation) compensatory; direct, indirect or consequential damages; loss of data, income or profit; loss of or damage to property, and claims of third parties and punitive damages.

Made in the USA
Columbia, SC
28 August 2018